There Are Things We Live Among

There Are Things We Live Among
Poems by Patrick Moran

GRAYSON BOOKS
West Hartford, CT
GraysonBooks.com

There Are Things We Live Among
copyright © 2016, Patrick Moran
Published by Grayson Books
West Hartford, Connecticut
Printed in the USA

Moran, Patrick (Poet), author.
  [Poems. Selections]
  There are things we live among : poems / by Patrick Moran.
  pages cm
  ISBN 978-0-9962809-3-8

  I. Title.

PS3613.O6824A6 2016   811'.6
                             QBI16-600010

ISBN: 978-0-9962809-3-8

Book & Cover Design by Cindy Mercier
Cover Images by Bethann Moran
Author Photo courtesy of Bethann Moran

GraysonBooks.com

Contents

Acknowledgements — viii

I
Nail Clippers — 11
Abacus — 12
Crutches — 13
Hook — 15
Coat Hangers — 16
Stairs — 17
Tweezers — 20
Radiators — 21
Dust — 22
Mouse Trap — 25
Knots — 26
Maps — 27
Cracks — 29
Cardboard Box — 30

II
Frost — 33
Tar — 35
Mold — 37
Sand — 38
Cobwebs — 39
Winter Orchard — 40
Maple — 41
Birches — 42
Ice Storm — 43
Tamarack Swamp — 44
Sapling — 45
Electrons — 46
Slivers — 48

III
Sun Glasses — 51
Handkerchief — 52

Comb	53
Mason Jar	54
Wire	55
Ghost Watch	56
Stick Matches	58
Closet	59
Wall	60
Corners	62
Windows	63
Chalkboard	64
Umbrella	66
Chimneys	67
Pins and Needles	68
Broken Plate	69
About the Author	70

Acknowledgements

Seneca Review: "Pins and Needles" & "Wire"
Notre Dame Review: "Ghost Watch"
Tar River Poetry Review: "Chimneys"
Northwest Review: "Tweezers"
Hayden's Ferry Review: "Crutches"
The Madison Review: "Umbrella"
The Sow's Ear Poetry Review: "Radiators" & "Stairs"
New Orleans Review: "Chalkboard"
ACM (Another Chicago Magazine): "Cardboard Box" & "Windows"
The Amherst Review: "Dust" & "Sun Glasses"
Pearl: "Mouse Traps"
The Whiskey Island Magazine: "Maps" & "Hook"
The New Republic: "Abacus"
Passages North: "Knots" & "Stick Matches"
Sulphur River Literary Review: "Closet"
New Laurel Review: "Corners"
Southern Poetry Review: "Cobwebs"
Farmer's Market: "Frost"
Sycamore Review: "Tar"
The Iowa Review: "Slivers"
Pegasus: "Sand" & "Mold"
Prairie Schooner: "Birches" & "Ice Storm"
Mid-America Review: "Nail Clippers"
Cumberland Review: "Tamarack Swamp" & "Broken Plate"
Green Mountain Review: "Coat Hangers"

Parts of "Electrons" were derived from Murray Gell-Mann's book, *The Quark and the Jaguar,* Little Brown 1994.

I.

There are things
We live among 'and to see them
Is to know ourselves'.

—George Oppen,
Of Being Numerous

Nail Clippers

Ventriloquist's dummy,
tiny chattering skull,

oily immigrant
from a knife factory,

Darwin wanted you
to have wings,

Pavlov kept you
under his pillow,

Jung placed you next to
his arrow heads.

Pearl-handled cocoon,
monogrammed mantis,

as possessions go
you exist in

the hierarchy of objects
somewhere between

the ice pick
& the C-clamp.

Son of the scissors,
daughter of the tooth,

night after night
you collect the moon

from our finger tips
one sliver at a time.

Abacus

Nephew of Daedalus
        counting your grains of sand,
                nervous, bookish pupil

of everything abstract,
        the bead & wire routine
                got you pretty far,

got you into the temple,
        gave the thinkers
                something to play with

besides their beards,
        gave them permission
                to ask how much is much?

& how many
        can many really be?
                & is more necessarily more

or is it a less complicated
        form of less? Suddenly
                zeros were a dime a dozen,

stars, termites & eternity
        scattered but negotiable
                & your secret name, *dust,*

was on everybody's lips.

Crutches

Hundreds of them
        hanging on the walls
                of a shop bolted shut
from the inside.
        Nobody on the streets,
                no wind in the trees,
something is happening
        in another part of town.
                Perhaps someone unimportant has died.
It should rain but it won't.
        They like it this way,
                this bored/heavy silence
that everything else
        must struggle through.
                Don't think they haven't noticed
the rising number of miracles
        or the remarkable absence
                of withered limbs
or the advancements made
        in the faith healing industry.
                Don't think they haven't
been disappointed with
        the disappearance of many
                gangrenous infections
or the recent decline in the military's
        production of amputees.
                It will be years before
a customer disturbs
        this sterilized picnic of strife,
                this quiz show for the insane,
this museum of bad breath.
        But when he drifts
                through the door,
a salesman from hell,
        a hallucinating gangster,
                a carp with a briefcase,

things will be like
         they were before--
                  a ship of happy cripples
blowing kisses in the rain.

Hook

Reserved:
   knows what to expect,
when to act,
   when to hang on.
Minds its own
   business,
speaks when it's spoken to,
   knows something
about cruelty,
   keeps it to itself.
The light
   is never kind
nor is it necessary.
   Glint is the only
word it knows.
   Standing still
it gives the impression
   of swinging,
the gentle rise
   & swell of space
surround it,
   tell it what to do.
On moonlit nights
   it feels like a crucifix,
the meat packers
   bow & pray.

Coat Hangers

Nearsighted,
self-conscious,

terribly disappointed
by fate,

by the conspiring
stillness

of a warm afternoon,
there is an Egyptian story

to tell,
a legend about

a hawk's head
twisted onto the body

of a scarab,
a camel's onto a crab.

Eventually
there is an escape,

then a period
of anonymity

followed by more
anonymity.

Stairs

Of two minds,
of two ideologies,

one ascending:
optimistic, willing,

prepared to trust,
almost blind.

The other a cynic:
descending,

suspicious,
ready to point

the finger,
giving to gravity

what would otherwise
be taken.

*

In darkness
they increase

or decrease
as they see fit.

In exhaustion
they alter angles

to hinder whomever
they please.

*

One step is for
the killer,

one step is for
the ghost,

one step is for
remembering,

One step is for
loss,

One step is for
turning & going

back the way
you came.

*

Blackened,
on the outside

of a building,
they are neither

appendage nor spine
but something

long extinct,
born a skeleton,

born black
& shuddering.

*

They know everything
about falling,

about the fatal
shifting

of one's weight.
They know

who pushed whom;
they know momentum

is its own
contrived form

of violence,
however brief.

*

One step is for
the killer,

one step is for
the ghost,

one step is for
remembering,

one step is for
loss,

one step is for
turning & going

back the way
you came.

Tweezers

Meticulous beak
of a bird

Our hands
the bald head

Our slivers
Our black hairs
its meager diet

Our skin
the place
to which it returns

again & again

As if in a darker
Epoch

of our human
History

We were once
covered
with feathers

Radiators

Never for very long,
far from urgent,
they begin their knocking

with no thoughts
or doors to open.
To say they are waking

from a river's dream
or an ocean's sleep
ignores the tin cup,

the dull bent spoon
they have somehow hidden
in the kennel of themselves.

This is not about rescuing
they seem to murmur,
you couldn't come here,

not this underworld,
no Eurydices weeping
for love's mismanaged myth.

Even now one only
half thinks about
their outward templeness,

columns cream-colored,
bone & silver:
little bureaucracies of dust

closed indefinitely
for repairs.

Dust

Because you
>breathe & move,
>>because we

breathe & move,
>because this is the only life
>>there is,

this drifting & swimming
>of lesser things,
>>because this life

of ours is yours,
>because we've come
>>from you,

because you surround
>our histories,
>>the famous, the infamous,

the tragic,
>& the otherwise,
>>there is no other way.

Because we will not know
>when you have left,
>>because you cling to mirrors

seeing everything
>but yourself,
>>because you are older

than the clothes
>whose odor you have
>>always been a part of,

because you hold
      certain houses
           in your quiet grip,

each locked room,
      each curtained window,
           the beds sagging with ghosts,

because you never
      intended to stay,
           because you are already

somewhere else,
      waiting there with vases
           & unopened letters,

with paintings,
      their darkness with whom
           you have already blended,

because you reveal yourself
      through neglect,
           through the white

finger tips of a glove,
      through rags
           whose lives roughly

resemble our own,
      because you have
           no other voice,

because what we are hearing
      is only our breath
           passing through

your thin-lipped silences,
      because you are kin
           to ashes, a cousin to dirt,

because you are
        a distant relative
                of silt & loam

& gun powder,
        because you singe
                in the company of matches,

flatten with
        the mystery of water,
                collect in the corners

like forgotten clouds,
        your embodiments,
                your configurations,

they are inevitable.
        Because even now
                as the light pools,

as the moon fades,
        as the trees drift
                a helpless dance of veils,

because even now
        someone is discovering you,
                is walking toward you,

is crossing a room
        for the first time,
                their hand,

it moves
        like an angel
                into this vision of light.

Mouse Traps

To them
        it is always
                the same mouse,
the same
        tentativeness,
                the same
delicate paws
        crossing
                the threshold,
& when
        the struggling
                stops
the same silence
        resuming
                its empty labors.
To them
        it is always
                the same night,
the same
        ignorant hour,
                the same
moonless,
        breathless
                soup kitchen,
the same
        delicate paws
                crossing
the threshold
        & when
                the struggling stops
the same
        silence resuming
                its empty labors.

Knots

Small heads
  crammed
with tiny visionary
  moments,
fists beating
  at the doors
of a stone.
  They can take care
of themselves,
  they can get themselves
out of jail,
  they can live
among the natives,
  they can live alone.
When they mate
  it's for life.
Courtship only occurs
  in the company
of sailors
  seconds before a mutiny.
They say
  it's like snakes
consuming themselves,
  like angels
wrestling in the lap
  of God.

Maps

are about being
in two places at once,

about looking
at where you are

but not seeing yourself.
They are about

seeing where you are going
but not seeing it

until you get there
& about seeing

where you were
but not seeing it either.

They are about
a bird's eye view

without having a bird's eye
or being a bird.

They are all about
pointing

& not pointing
at what isn't the place

& what is.
The whole issue

of large becoming small
doesn't seem

to bother anyone nor does
the extreme absence

of people seem to faze
its inhabitants.

The old ones,
drawn from memory,

always had a leviathan
in the more remote reaches.

In its own way
the fish-eyed monstrosity

seemed to be saying
there is an incalculable

risk involved,
a terrible price to be paid

for looking at what
you will never see,

for moving toward
the as yet unimagined

without any proof
of it being there.

Many consider
the most accurate maps

to be drawn in the sand
with a stick

or in the palm of a small hand
with a dirty finger.

Cracks

The simultaneity
        of spoil & bloom:
                curiosity
as a means to an end.
        Distant relative
                to the river,
following them
        is madness
                once removed.
God regrets.
        The angels look
                away.
They came
        with the territory,
                with the desire
for mass.
        All of their questions
                are rhetorical.
There is a distinct
        dryness
                to their speech,
a hollowness
        alluding to bone,
                to the pure
silence of marble,
        to the consciousness
                of the egg
who knows them
        as the disciples
                of the most
holy Shiva.

Cardboard Box

No one seems
        to remember
                just where
you came from
        or how you
                came to be
so full
        of the past.
                Even the printed
fruit foolishly
        smiling
                under
an exhausted sun
        seems
                to be just
another
        empty incarnation.
                Strange
the way
        you reduce
                our lives,
becoming
        the destination
                for the precious,
the unnecessary,
        the purely
                sentimental,
the way we
        concede
                & conform,
as if you
        knew all along
                that this is all
we would
        ever amount to.

II.

If one day you see
that a pebble is smiling at you

will you go and tell?

—Eugene Guillevic

Frost

We kill
        tomatoes & raspberries,
pumpkin & squash,
        whole orchards
of whatever you want.
        We are precise,
turning the dew
        into a crust of white;
we are meticulous,
        seeping into the grass
deadening each
        hair-like root.
Never mind
        the windows, the stalks
of blackening corn,
        we've transformed
the soil into stone,
        the cul-de-sac
of the river
        into unbreakable glass.
If we are, in fact,
        an army, we are
the faceless foot soldiers
        without bayonets,
without bullets
        brutally successful
despite ourselves.
        As the agents
of fissure & flaw
        we are incapable
of missing weakness;
        driving our
microscopic wedges
        further & further
we move
        beyond boundaries
& brittle thought.
        Brush your hand

against our accumulations,
 you will only
find more.
 Yes, you will have left
your mark, but we will
 have made it ours.

Tar

My somber mood
is unshakable.

I am the pessimist's
pessimist.

If I thought
it would change things

I would wear
a sandwich board

around my neck
proclaiming

"THE END IS NEAR!"
All my ballads

are in a minor key.
All my stories end

with the most
tragic conclusion,

everything dies
even the plants.

I revel in death's
inevitability.

It's drawn to me
like the flies,

the Wooly Mammoth,
the great Irish Elk

& those lumbering,
absent-minded dinosaurs.

Their wailing
& suffering

were monumental,
epic in proportion,

Wagnerian. I have
learned to be patient,

that haste makes waste,
that there is no rest

for the wicked
& only one way

to skin a cat.
I am familiar

with punishment
& the way justice

creates a window
for cruelty.

As for the feathers
I want to say

they were an afterthought,
but I can't really

explain it &
that bothers me.

Mold

Politely, quietly,
   discreetly, while
your back was turned,
   in your absence,
before your eyes,
   we've made ourselves
at home, blooming
   & blossoming;
encouraged by the air,
   by the damp, by
the lack of light---
   like tiny displaced
cornflowers, buds
   of sweet William,
hoary little violets;
   if we move at all
it is with extreme
   elegance, like clouds
covering the moon.

Sand

Got a caravan to get rid of?
        a prophet whose mouth needs stuffing?
Or maybe you want a pyramid
        unloosed from its moorings?
Is there a city that needs to disappear?
        a name that must be forgotten?
Or perhaps you are waiting
        for us to drag the sphinx out to sea
& drown it like a kitten.

Cobwebs

encrusted with dust
devastated by light

at the mercy
of the breeze

constantly in danger
afraid of being

interrupted mid-sentence
mid-thought

our gentle architectures
quietly at risk

carefully watching
for an opportunity

an opening
we are secretly planning

for the worst
we are curtains

we are tapestries
we are nightgowns

gone mad

Winter Orchard

backs bent, limbs lifted
we are the ones who wait

because waiting is the way
marching, not marching

in our gun-metal skins
backs bent, limbs lifted

dead white disc of the sun
not even bothering to rise

because waiting is the way
mad clattering of crows

keeping us a company,
backs bent, limbs lifted

oh black flags, black flowers
refusing to open over the snow

because waiting is the way
we are guards, we are prisoners

all waiting for the escape
backs bent, limbs lifted

because waiting is the way

Maple

Call me a green cloud
of sparrows making passionate love,
a brothel of leaves,

a den of rustling inequities,
so cool, so exquisite.
Listen to me murmur

phrases from Omar Khayyam,
listen to the green horses
toss like an ocean,

a green locomotive chugging
softly across the night bridge.
Left to my own devices

I might become a peeping Tom,
a shameless voyeur;
just stealing glances,

there & here,
a child in a crib, a girl
with a towel around her head

looking endlessly into a mirror.
My shyness soon fades,
soon I will be staring, brazenly,

studying even the most
private details: the woman
painting her toenails,

a new mole on her thigh.
In a fit of boldness I might
scratch the roof or tap the window,

& then, with a storm
as my excuse, I'd come crashing,
violent, wanting, mad.

Birches

We are the ghostly veins
across the lake,

our kin lie at
our feet; you are

thinking of us as chalk.
Our hearts rot

before our skins---
it makes us ruthless;

our sturdiness,
our alabaster complexions,

our pillar impressions
in the wilderness,

they mean nothing.
With or without the wind

we will fall: a wet
sound, a splitting

of skin, a crash
of little or no consequence.

Unmourned, in pieces
on the ground

our dead still possess
the rare elegance

of stolen statues.
They stare at the sky

as we bury them with leaves.

Ice Storm

On glass beads,
on veneered feet,

on pikestaffs,
on thorns,

on purpose,
on course:

a perfect net
all scales & shine,

all spoons
& knives,

polish & sheen,
burnishings

bejeweled & aglare,
I am the last

terrible queen!!!

Tamarack Swamp

It's our job
to look dead,
stand as if it
were our
last wish,
our condemned
calling.
Thin as prisoners
in this gulag
of eel grass,
we bide our
time sipping
the bitter rations
of our internment:
the rinds
& the skins
of those who've
gone before us.
Think of us
as ghosts,
houses haunted
by branches,
roots & limbs,
the ground
cursed &
the sky clawed
with light.
Upon entering
it's your worried
heart we hear
sounding these
empty depths,
not your footsteps,
not your breath,
but your heart.

Sapling

Like your memory
   of a niece, I am
forever small,
   unobtrusive, polite,
my awkward
   appearances not
worth acknowledging.
   Glove-like &
tissue-thin,
   my shy allotment
of leaves unfold
   & unfurl. I will
stand like a comb,
   like a hair brush,
like a hand mirror.
   I will look as if
I am waiting,
   as if I am watching,
as if I've been
   stood up for
the only date
   I will ever have.

Electrons

We are the ones
for whom somewhere else is a place

we must always be rushing off to
where everything true is always true

& for whom somewhere else is a place
from moment to moment

where everything true is always true
& nothing is contingent

from moment to moment
where the exquisite is beyond repair

& nothing is contingent
where one plus one is a jaguar

& the exquisite is beyond repair
& nowhere is where we are

where one plus one is a jaguar
& two plus two is another jaguar

which is nowhere & where we are
accidents springing from complexity

as two plus two is another jaguar
in another forest

accidents springing from complexity
& nothing will be forgotten

in another forest
where being right is not enough

because nothing will ever be forgotten
& we must always be rushing off to

where being right is not enough
& we are the ones

Slivers

Knives without handles,
pins without heads,

needles void
of that one graceful eye,

we can hold out
for weeks in the village

of your thumb,
in the country of your hand.

III.

world world world world
and the face grave
cloud against the evening

—Samuel Beckett

Sun Glasses

Don't look now
>but they're all watching,
>>calculating your next move,

making intricate plans.
>Don't try to join them either.
>>It's too late for that.

Just pretend they're tourists
>trying to place your face
>>or insurance salesmen

suddenly at a loss for words.
>If they ask for directions
>>point west or claim

you are like them,
>only a stranger passing through.
>>If they persist & want to talk

about the weather
>oblige them, they will soon
>>run out of words

& digress into meaningless gestures.
>As the sun disappears
>>only a few of the fervent ones

will remain on the streets.
>Nervously turning their heads,
>>suddenly unsure

of their whereabouts,
>they will begin running
>>as if they are being consumed

by flames.
>Stay out of their way.

Handkerchief

Companion
Mon Frere
You are a road map

Of tears, snot
& sweat
You are a chamber

Of coughs
A harbor
Of brown & red spit

Grand depot
Of the infinite sneeze
Second class nobody

In the breast pocket
Of a corpse
White as a tooth

You are the ticket
The almighty boarding pass
To that mysterious

other shore

Comb
for Kenny

Only the barber
   knows your loneliness,
your hayseed wisdom,
   your quiet fortitude.
In his white
   institutional tunic,
at the end of
   an eternal Tuesday,
he is wistful because
   the love of his life
has not broken
   the heel of her shoe
outside his door
   for yet another day,
& so he tells you again
   the unspeakable color
of her bright red hair.

Mason Jar

        Quiet chapel of dreams
by which someone
        is just now reading
a letter in the light of,
        an often folded letter
from another war,
        a letter the color of old skin,
the light curiously warm,
        the careless light,
the absentminded light,
        the kind that wakes you
from a sound sleep
        to stand naked in front of,
not remembering
        how you got there
or why you are holding
        a jar in each hand or what
you should do next.

Wire

Malleable, yes,
curious about the future,
              never.
Doesn't give it
a second thought.

Doesn't give it
the time of day.
              Not when
there are so many
rose heads to hold up,
so many
posable dolls to pose.

The fact is,
that it's busy
being paper clips, bread ties,
pipe cleaners,
              bicycle brakes.

It helps when you don't
have a conscience
or an abiding sense
        of your own
                mortality.

Somehow, though,
it has retained
this ruthless streak,
              a crooked
appearance,
there poking
though the fabric
of the too-much-loved-toy
              or sleeved in

the blues & the reds
of a working bomb.

Ghost Watch

To look
        & see nothing
                confirms its presence.
To rub & find
        only a dampness
                admits the impossible.
There where
        the arm ends,
                where the hand begins,
the pulse
        of its mechanisms
                undermining the skin's
ability to forget,
        deferring the bone's
                longing for release.
It knows all about
        that construct
                we like to call time,
those increments
        of increments
                stacked so neatly
in the air.
        Like all ghosts
                it haunts with a purpose,
& like all ghosts
        it must obey
                certain prescribed laws.
There are no
        palpable murders
                it seeks to revenge,
no ancestral curses
        it wishes to absolve;
                it is after something
much finer,
        as subtle as
                the almost invisible

colorless hairs
  that retain its impression
    like a memory.
Then it's gone
  & because
    there is nothing remarkable
about its absence,
  no residue,
    no chill,
the light somehow
  exactly the same,
    we try to think,
to understand
  that some things are
    purely errands
performed
  in the void,
    then that's gone too.

Stick Matches

Little volunteers, red & blue helmets,
        Who is in charge?
Who is at the command post?
        & why has the radio been dead for so long?
Such a curious silence,
        the kind that waits to be broken,
the kind that whispers
        the names it is afraid to say out loud.

What has not been explained by the fine print
        will be explained by the finer print.
What has been left to the imagination
        will have its mouth washed out with soap.
Ant-like in their restless preparations,
        business-like in their rigorous uniforms,
they keep asking
        the same hopeless question.
Now? Now? Now?

Closet

Think of it
   as a lounge,
quiet, dim,
   a handful of regulars
near the door,
   older, thinner
clientele
   near the back.
Or perhaps
   as the greenroom
to which the actors
   always return,
without
   the body's drama
to stand simply
   as they were.
One wants
   to say something
about skeletons,
   feels impelled
by their presence,
   by the gentleness
of their hands.
   Closing the door,
you feel them
   pushing
at what they know
   cannot stay
silenced forever.

Wall

    Waiting for a painting
as a point of departure,
    waiting for a window
to see where you are,
    waiting for a shelf
because meaning is an emblem,
    waiting for a mirror
because desire never ends.

    Permanent or temporary,
voices comply to your wishes;
    sounds stall or dissolve
according to your laws.
    Concealment is one of your many
rules & functions.
    While ignorance thickens,
knowledge smashes
    the occasional hole.

Whitewashed & scrubbed
    you came into the world
with a clear conscience;
    once you might have blushed
or averted your gaze
    from the mongrels humping
in the alley way
    but that was long before
the convict made you his calendar
    or the clock its home.

Those who have turned
    their faces toward you,
who have peered into
    your wintry distances
always seem to be looking
    for the same thing.

Adjusting & readjusting
  their vision to your squalls
& disturbances,
  they stare with a statue's
attention to detail,
  with the secret amusement
of certain unwanted dolls.

Corners

Only the punished
truly understand
the richness
of their symmetry,
the severe
dualities of east
meeting west,
of left touching right.
Only the confined
experience
the precise deprivation
of space as line
follows line
toward the point
of perfect singularity.
They say the game
of being insane
has no arguable rules,
that the fluctuation
of angles
cannot be proved.
They say for every corner
there is a spider
who is the prisoner,
a fly who is
the jailer
& a vanishing point
from which
no one ever returns.

Windows

Such
a fragile race
of trembling nobodies.
Such a nervous
surface of shimmer
& sheen.
Such imperfect
reflectors of sky,
bodies & darkness.
Watch them
unpack their cutlery,
their glacial razors,
their tailored
shark skin suits
when brick
& mannequin meet
themselves
coming & going
like divers
reflected
in a frozen pool.

Chalkboard

There is relevance
        to struggle with,
                a dilemma over

the meaning of marks
        made & unmade;
                there is the universe

of its surface to deal with,
        at once dark & starless
                then suddenly

illuminated with
        equations & cursive.
                It can't compete

with the drama
        of the windows or the doors
                or the liberating silences

of the ceiling.
        It assumes therefore
                a much more

transparent
        & classical demeanor:
                there when it's there

& not there when its there.
        In our dreams of them
                we are always children,

we can somehow
        see ourselves at the edge
                of its greenish shores

& also feel
        the weight of the chalk
                like a smooth stone

that we can't bring ourselves
        to skip or
                throw away just yet.

Umbrella

Oh skinny bones,
        oh cheap date,
Who has offended you
        this time?
Who called your mother
        a pterodactyl knockoff?
Who called your father
        a broken down
chrysanthemum?
        Listen, your swan days
are numbered.
        Your enemies know
what you're up to.
        There's a gust of wind
out there with your
        name on it.
& if things weren't bad enough,
        your precious little brood
has found their way
        to the cocktail lounge.
You're not going to like
        what you see.

Chimneys

If a house burns down
        they have to be
                the last one standing,
towering over the ashes
        in the charred cloak
                of a mourner.
If bodies have to be burned,
        they are the ignorant
                accomplices looking,
always looking
        the other way.
                At night they can lose
themselves among the stars,
        they can pretend
                we don't exist,
that it's just them
        commiserating with the moon.
                But in the morning
if the wind is right,
        theyr'e all plumes, banners,
                bed sheets, curlicues,
or the long, white scarf
        of a dead hero
                no one can seem to recall.

Pins and Needles

    Whoever said
they were mortal enemies
had it all wrong,
    had misunderstood

    the complex relationship
of master and servant,
of heart & head.
    Whoever said

    they were loners, drifters
& transients
forgot that they work
    late into the night

    squinting for hours
at the intricacies
of a long lost design.
    Whoever said

    they had no hand
in our destiny,
no interest in our fate,
    our well-being,

    never accepted
an apple from a stranger.
So red, so inviting,
    you would swear

it was filled with blood.

Broken Plate

il en faut ramasser les debris
—Jean Follain

Freed from its servitude
it no longer thinks

of water or the hands
of a girl who held it

while someone tried
to kiss her.

It no longer thinks
of the wedges of lemon

floating in the beaded
water glasses

or how the other body,
not quite a ghost,

came to be
so close to the girl's.

Each bead of water seemed
a world unto itself

& the bright yellow
wedge a sun,

& the kiss, the plate
no longer thought,

had been either her first
or her last.

About the Author

Patrick Moran is the author of four collections of poetry: *Tell A Pitiful Story*, *Doppelgangster*, *The Book of Lost Things*, and *Rumors of Organized Crime*. His poetry, essays, and translations have appeared in many journals and publications including *The New Republic*, *Crazyhorse*, *The Writer's Chronicle*, and the *Tampa Review*. He is currently a professor of creative writing at the University of Wisconsin-Whitewater.